COLD-PRESS MOON

COLD-PRESS MOON

Dennis Cooley

TURNSTONE PRESS

cold-press moon
copyright © Dennis Cooley 2020

Turnstone Press
Artspace Building
206-100 Arthur Street
Winnipeg, MB
R3B 1H3 Canada
www.TurnstonePress.com

All rights reserved. No part of this book may be reproduced or transmitted in any form or by any means—graphic, electronic or mechanical—without the prior written permission of the publisher. Any request to photocopy any part of this book shall be directed in writing to Access Copyright, Toronto.

Turnstone Press gratefully acknowledges the assistance of the Canada Council for the Arts, the Manitoba Arts Council, the Government of Canada through the Canada Book Fund, and the Province of Manitoba through the Book Publishing Tax Credit and the Book Publisher Marketing Assistance Program.

Earlier versions of some of these poems have appeared in the chapbook *Goldfinger*. Others have appeared in the journals *jacket 2*, *CV2*, and the *Winnipeg Free Press*.

Cover image: Winter Moon by Hanna Arnason McNeil

Printed and bound in Canada.
Library and Archives Canada Cataloguing in Publication

Title: Cold-press moon / Dennis Cooley.
Names: Cooley, Dennis, 1944- author.
Description: Poems.
Identifiers: Canadiana (print) 20190233680 | Canadiana (ebook) 20190233699 | ISBN 9780888016737 (softcover) | ISBN 9780888016744 (EPUB) | ISBN 9780888016751 (Kindle) | ISBN 9780888016768 (PDF)
Classification: LCC PS8555.O575 C65 2020 | DDC C811/.54—dc23

for Diane, Dana, and Megan
with thanks to Rob Budde for his thoughtful advice

Contents

I: Gold Finger

II. Two-Thirds of the Sun

III: The Lost Children

IV: Rapunzel
    garrison mentality / 45
    Mother Gothel / 47

V: The Bear
    the girls and the bear / 61
    the bear and the frog / 70

VI: The Frog and the Princess
    she kisseth the amphibian / 75
    the father, aghast, contemplates her choices / 77
    the father confers with the queen / 80
    the frog & the princess / 84

VII: Goldilocks

VIII: Snow White
    mirror / 93
    snow white, her complexion / 99
    snow white, dancing / 101

IX: Victorian Romance
    planting / 107
    frankenstein seeks donor / 113
    the word you say / 115

X: By the River Sticks
    he dies in the hands / 127

XI: Once Bitten
    he is born / 139
    obstetrics / 140
    in the flying machine / 142
    he considers astrophysics / 143
    it's our slinky way of walking / 144
    they go boating / 146
    listen / 148
    something in my eyes / 150
    Mina Harker / 152
    they find their tongues / 154
    old times' sake / 156

COLD-PRESS MOON

I: Gold Finger

I

i come to her in darkness they say I shine and they are
afraid they say they close up in their eyes they feel my
skin full of holes a leather that hangs from cold some say
I have heard them say they can hear winter in my heart a
wind they duck my shortness and they sprinkle salt look
mum the funny man when I pass *shh sshh* it's nothing
dear even the geese cringe turn cool as shadows by the
well where the creosote holds water shrinks & I dream of
her dream I saw her at the mill I am sure she did not see
me at the bottom of the water I am lost among the goats
and ducks think I am a white dwarf a crate of rickets the
crickets click and drip & bugs that form in flour bite and
yet they need me have lost G2 in the village they say the
king is dull and pale they call him cowardly and they
sense I might help have seen me do tricks with string
seen a comet sizzle in the seas and the pigs have sore feet

II

In the prison of darkness I come to her all night *whirr whirr* I watch the poisson swim in the poisoned well my darkness a passion swims I crack open the hinges on cold slip through nights smooth as a mussel she hides in for her father the miller has fooled the king has told him the maiden can spin night into gold you must not cut off her hands she can draw gold filament after filament from the wheel and she weeps weeps she cannot think or sleep my lady pines and sticks pins in the back of her hand she stings herself until morning gathers from the corners darkness makes and smears on the window and wipes it up she hums & she sings drinks brandy oh yes her father the miller does not know nor the king who wants her fibres of gold that unfold in ribbons and bolts does not know she drinks brandy in a ferment weeps for me she waits under the bridge in the fraunhofer lines where I watch still as a frog and inside as smooth though she does not know already I have her ring and necklace also the night songs she dripped into the room *blip blip* one by one it is all I have she said to me she could hardly breathe but I know there is more and I am waiting I have sealed time behind the clang where the door closes shut and she weeps

III

I come to her in darkness I am an eel slither darkness
the spools of night she has fallen in stiff as stone echo
all the way to the stables and the elation in the king's
dressing room into empty ears she weeps it is deep the
darkness curves back on itself an elbow in the night I
swim I will one day win her swim into her tears she will
look up from the book and see I am beautiful look lady
look I too can turn things into fine skeins of light bright
& fine as her hair they will catch her night tears where
they have bled and in the morning from the first rivulet
of sun I will pull them up two moons into my boat one
by one they will glisten in my hands they will be shivery
with silver and gold I will sweep them over the bow into
the bowl the bed I have prepared I will spin and spin, the
wheel will reel like the constellations for her for my uncle
the king held her the king held her down & he spat into
her mouth & now a flame shudders through & things
spurt from her mouth near & far as words we do not
know he wants only gold wants only what he thinks she
can bring him when I bring him her I bring her to me
spin love all night long sing of how pleased she will spin
pins and mother-of-all she will sing the world on its axis
quickly whirl the seven sisters into knots fine nets strings
of pisces on her great bales of straw she holds and weeps
for joy he snips she will not be killed in her eyes I look
for some sign but I cannot tell it is sunset a cold wind
blowing rain from the north hard on the snow fences and
into our faces and the trails the children go on are spoiled

IV

I come to her in darkness slide through the door on a
small muscle of must call to her lady lady I call and call
but she does not always hear I am what happens when
she thinks my name a pebble at the tip of her tongue
I am in and i spit in her mouth a hot spot of mercury
stops my thoughts sizzle at the tips of memory the little
dabs of heat she does not know who I am she does not
care though she does not draw back who are you as at
first she must have smelled me small as hope or the key
on the door the first night when I came to her weeping
black tears for she must have wept then from the mills of
cold though I did not look did not look away from where
I found the ends of ropes badly frayed and pulled them
and scraped my fingers on the cold they hold her in and
bobbing threw them reams and reams into that shiver
she must have wept slept even as I piled stacks and stacks
of sun soft as earthworms breath we could hear the cold
rumble and melt she must have known I had combed the
moon fleeced the sky could not have failed to see I would
die for her and king betelgeuse drunk unaware wanting
only the yarn that glowed in her hands I mined from
night

she could hardly see at first laughed over the threads you have done it you have done it and the blood leapt to her face she knew she could climb out and she looked at me as others do soon she will see I am blue my fingertips are blue I am a blue flame and when I slip into her room I flare it is true I shine and when I do little blups of light escape from my throat through the holes in it and my whole body aches with a light so hot she cannot see or enter

V

and yet I come to her in darkness do not care that she
knows my name do not mind I turn for her the kings
gold do not care even when after I have her necklace and
next her ring do not want really the child she desperate
weeping promises at the treadle bent over want only she
will find some crevice where my bones will bloom and
my skin oh my lady for you I reel night into morning all
night sing to the strings on the dream I spin for you the
clacking mill the open gate where we feed the geese over
my darkness you swim your spine of light

II. Two-Thirds of the Sun

❋

      everything a haze heat a slur across
                my face everything
    a blaze, the smell of spruce in heat

      leave the others at the foot the horses
        jangling, flies shiver, horses grazing.
  Michael and the others sing, sip beer, talk.
              Gaze at me as I was
                  told they would.

Pull my curiosity my future
up the rocks, up the mountain
climb until the moon is a wheel
in my hand hold the round feel of it
            at 830

hand over hand I pulley my blood up
until it turns rubbery
slouches in lopsided grin

body a hot water bottle I haul
at the end of a yo-yo moon
its wide-open yawn saw the moon
throw a rope around tomorrow
& hoist it up the wall

Climb all evening, all night long,
for what I may find, and fear I will.

    The woman still reaching for the udder,
    the young man, wart on his left cheek,
    about to pull hairs out of the curry comb.
    The chicken stopped in mid-step,
    rust stuck in its throat,
    the pump's water music seized up.
    A pail almost spilled from the kitchen
    window stopped in mid-air, amazed,
    100 years ago the fire fallen
    asleep the spider about to bite
    the fly howling in silken finery,
    every thing held inside its breath.

    the start of recognition painted into the girl's face.

Even the wind. The wind swallows itself,
like a bottle. The place is a spider
on the bottom of a line forever
dropped from our dreams.

❋

have heard the stories we all know how
the wise women came and blessed
the child and a thirteenth left
out because there was no room
no plate for her there were only twelve.
Left out left over she takes what is left to her,
they always do, the thirteenth, and the other,
resenting the young beauty.
A story into which the girl is taken
falls dead at fifteen, falls dead from a prick.
Yes, that is what the story says.

        I did not write it.
         Nor did you.
       We have only to read
        as it was written.

   Only they don't tell that part
   they say I am a figure
   who wears power in his belt
   sticks privilege like a feather
   into his hat.

I tell you how I hack my way
through thorns how thorns turn
into flowers part as I walk through
past bodies of young men impaled
torn open under the moon's bright eye

they have thrown themselves on the barb
wire life is held in or out by.

They don't tell you how they lay there
dried fruit dried flowers dozens of them
juiced out sucked empty
how their eyes are pecked out by crows
as they are drying into paper,
the privilege of death their bodies assume
on the way to a briar cemetery.

Nor do they tell how uncanny as dream
the palace lies without moving
not a bit of air along the wet walls
so near death so close to me and far

—walk inside my body's sounds
the assurance of the bones & muscles
whip of clothes against clothes
bodies dripping from time like banners
my clothes snap when I walk by
I can hear a moth walking in this cloud
this unknowing.
      Think of Michael, waiting.

✻

                    I know what they say
          that I come, male, a smile poised
            inside my rights sweep the pale
             girl onto her feet where when
                she wakes she weeps.

You know the impediments of thorns,
smile, knowing I should enter through flowers.
Some of you say she is comatose,
preserved rose, perfect emblem of what I seek,
see my arrival only as violation,
pleasure taken, power proven.

✻

                    This is what I find:

whinnies fall out of the horses
in spilled stones scatter at my feet,
shiver where flies surprise
as if they had never stopped the fire
gasps again against its breath the dogs leap
into barks they chase the chickens
        that walked their century
          old dream head-bobbing in the dream
         for the dogs for the chickens
step down into scratch & cluck slightly dazed

the mill goes *click clack click clack*
as if it cannot believe it is turning
the ducks gather up their feathers
follow them back into the shade that drops
from the sudden walls behind
        they have switched the sun on
        into the yard the release of dream from dream
        they all look at me look
        at one another shake themselves
        loose their bodies unlock, pop,
        they could be buttons coming
        undone their eyes snap open
        as if they had just remembered
                the world might unhinge
                might move again before wind
                grinds open against green

        ✼

but before that this is what happens:
                          I lean over to kiss
the lips cold as an ossuary
yet I must do this this
is why I have come why
i was sent
you insist that i do

Perhaps the young men tried to break through
that the roast might sizzle, the flies might crawl
that men & women might meet in stables
that girls in scullery might eat fried drumsticks
children collect stones and string
that people might wade through time
wake in time to time happening
over & over again.

Know only the old man said
you must kiss her you must
kiss the briar girl he said
when you find her years from now
in tears they will tell stories on you
and yet you must do this.

You will not want to do this the old man said
and he is right, I do not want to.
It doesn't help when I find the girl
frog-belly white from the years that drained her
tartared teeth, clothes soaked with water,
her face stained, mineral deposits on a pump,
and I could be back with Michael, drinking, talking.
                      stories of horses & music & women

❈

Lean over the wax, lethargic as a slug,
answer to chemicals the world swirls within,
  a cold mucous to awaken
  she does not want this either wants
  only to sleep to lie still
  simple as aether
  to be winter
  to be no more
  than wind when it is clear
  there is no wind

Blow on the others too, though they are
not pleased either, altogether,
I blow their stillness off them
cause them to move, waken them into death.

❈

Have only this excuse, that I have
left my friends down the hill that fields
when they turn over smell of earth
and in fall of wheat ripening

                    this is why I do it that milk
                 maids might milk that cows give milk
               that at night when the moon is out cows jump
                              each month floods
                            reliable as a carburetor
                          oestrus erupts, bloody egg,

                            do it for the family of red
                           wing black birds that drop
                                into the marshes
                              every summer to feed

                                       ✸

                       do it because it brings us around
                              two-thirds of the sun
                           because when the moon closes
                                 its eye I watch
                            the mascara of your sleeping

III: The Lost Children

THE WAIT

His children he knows are just on the other side, a thin membrane, and they bring their faces up to his. When he removes his glasses to read what is written there, the father is stricken.

something slips, somewhere inside, fish in dark water.

the father perhaps would light up. he was getting somewhere, a clear wick in a wet world, and he would quaver in the enormous fields of electricity Hansel and Gretel would surely see.

Then. Huge man with one eye, mean & twitchy. What will the father do? He's looking for jack, maybe you spotted him, little fella, yea high.

in the giant's brain a cricket is eating
it tastes a lot like a bean
the brain is turning to chaff

go on, go by, the father silent, to himself.
a dream, a charm.
a passing

THE COLD

has culled them from summer
the sky bleak and the wet snow falls

the stringy smells of cellars
boiled cabbage and turnips
the sour old woman
thick odour of her spit

in their clothes and they remember
the wire fences their hands froze on
the charred oven going night and day

    and now this
the bold beak in the flesh
dead robins on the road and squirrels squashed
the wires sprawled into the forest
where they live, the brother & sister & father.

They wait for their father's voice that will tilt the night and squeeze it down like a garbage compressor. We ourselves want the tricks when he talks to animals and spooks stones from spells that lie at the bottom of wells, inside walls, expect stray cows that amble to his call.

We wait, for this is a story of waiting. They wait for the yellow birds, the ocean of light he will whisk from his heart. The gravelly sprawl on the shores.

it swishes whishes
his heart releases onto
the edges of home, a giant
saucer on which his heart
like a cup rattles.

What chemistry to save them, or alchemy of love?

THE ESCAPE

They are out. The hot house behind them, they run into the blind night, their eyebrows, the fine hairs on their arms, feel the heat. Run from the old lady who pinches Hansel and leers. "Run Gretel, run." And they run, their little legs run, from the sugar and starch, the treacle in the old lady's voice. She is brittle as bone china, as watches with smashed faces that droop and tick, and glass in heat and cold blackens and cracks and smoke screams into the air.

They are out. The darkness stumbling, the adrenalin slings them. The cold slams against their faces sticky with fear and the old woman's spittle.

"Run Hansel, run." And they run.

They run and they run. Night streams under them and over them the stars spread like shrapnel in the frozen air eyes and breath through teeth the trees groan and tighten. Run till they can no longer, and they stop, gasping, drugged as lovers. Their faces are covered with nicks and smudges, their hands cut, and off the paths in the trees something wetly sparks and lowers.

The children catch their breath, they have it, their breath, the breath they chased into the night, from the hot house, over night. Their hearts are grouse drumming.

They shiver, they are alone.

"Wish Daddy were here."

Sounds of stars falling and going out. Scent of burnt wood. Blown-out lanterns, damp ashes. The moon floats on a pan of dark water.

"Gretel?"

"Yeah."

They can hear the great birds sleeping, talking to the night. They are alone and cold and far from home and it is dark and dark and dark.

The little boy and girl hunch down into their aloneness.

Bugs glow through the blue oil. The children can see a big eye at the hole, the enormous eye of the witch, and she is sucking light in a waterfall that runs backwards. She drags the shaggy roar back into her throat, she is sucking all the warmth out of them, and their hearts go slow as rocks on ice.

They hold one another closely. The air is clogging. They crouch under the cold and cry for their father. "Vati, vati," they call, softly. They hope he will hear as always at home he had spoken gently when they saw strange shapes bulging into the room. *Shsh shh-hh-hh* he had said on their shoulders, his voice low. *Shh.* The two small children weep for what they have left and for themselves, for the thoughts that once slept with them, warmly at night, at home.

They weep for love when it isn't there. They fall back from the frosts in the forest. The air is thick, so blue they cannot move.

They hope for the marigold that the grackles have not beheaded, maybe it will break open the sky. They want more than anything the warm blankets their mother had once brought to them.

A voice. But what? The rock they lean against begins to glow and they press themselves against it, it feels warm, it feels good against their backs.

"What is it, is it our Daddy?"

Smells of wheat and something fresh as new-mown hay. The earth eases, warm and sweet. Fresh bread and tea.

The cold begins to dissolve. The rust melts away and it is their father's voice in the big yellow rock they can hear.

"Daddy, Daddy," they cry. They cry for their father who is not there and for themselves who are.

The stone sings like a stove into the night. The children hold it between them and warm their hands on it.

"Listen."

"What? What, what? I can't hear. What is it?"

At their feet—little blips of light glisten from the light they carry between them, bright as a lantern and as warm.

They will follow the lights at their feet, and the Christmas lights too, slung on the sweet-smelling pines all the way home.

THE FATHER

the stones at night urge the seas in the father's body to the beach. He steps into shadows that form in the shapes of ships and enormous birds. He becomes a wind so high and so terrible he can hear the swish of his own blood, feels it mist on his face and the big yellow stone slides bright as mercury behind birds that make sounds of metal ripping.

my children, my children. The father's voice sounds like corn ripped open.

They run and fall run and fall, two small creatures. Near them animals bulge and make hoarse sounds. The children are lost and they listen. They hear the blood gone sour in the leaves the trees breathing hard the smell of goats and the wet snow on the cattle that stumble. The father fears his children are alone as the moon and as cold.

i will light a fire, children, for the forests are furred with frost.

There are rumours, strange tumours, far from home the night air charged. The sounds warp and howl. The father fears Hansel and Gretel may die alone and very far from home.

listen listen my children
    i am coming
           listen

THE RETURN

Night wind. A moon. Rain at the window.
The porch light clicks on, offers its little planet of warmth.
And now, children. Up the walk.
Running.
Children running.
The father looks up, sees. Them, his children. Hansel and Gretel, running.

The father calls. *Hansel, Gretel.* His voice on the cold night. *Hansel, Gretel.*

There is a high whooshing and they are running, it is raining the colour of colostrum.

Car lights moving in rain, lay down cellophane before them, bright red entrails they drag behind, beautiful in the film that runs through his head. They leave phosphorescent slugs stuck to the curbs, the drains, the eaves running over. Light splashes where he walks & stops, walks & stops, sticks the weak light from his hand out into the night. His children.

Then he is running too and the children. Dragging their broken wings, all three, up the road, down the road, up the stones the moon the wind the slap slap of their steps the steep rain in their faces their suddenness splashing and running, together, toward. Water in the curbs. Tears.

The father too, the father weeps. He weeps for his children and for himself and for sidewalks that hold feet up, for all the lost children running & running. Their mothers and fathers and the children his own childhood lost parents the stories they told that held the stars in their constellations fallen out of the horizon gone now into small voices under snow.

There is a high wind a high high wind and they are running and it is raining in their faces, their faces are raining.

THE FUNCTIONS

The father is not sure where he stands. He knows there can be changes to the story. Someone will dispatch, someone will depart, though we cannot be sure who. He is pretty sure his second wife has sent the children away and he knows with a hurt he cannot say they are gone. He knows the story may be reduced or expanded. Events may be inverted and some details may be corrupted. A prolepsis here, an analepsis there, but he's still the father, isn't he? He still loves his children. He has been in the story long enough to know there are substitutions and assimilations. This has been going on for a long time. Some of the emendations are archaic, some confessional. Some seem to come from religious impulses and others from literary.

He is not sure what Cooley will do. For there are functions and Cooley must reckon with them. Let Cooley play with the events and the sequence of events. The father can live with that. What bothers him are the 31 functions—the parts where the hero struggles with the villain, the parts where there are victims and villains. The magic agents act much as always they have. They are constant in malfeasance, resolute in intercession. This is a fairy tale and they are useful.

Is he himself, the father wonders, hero as donor, hero or villain? He has always believed he was good, stood between his children and hurts that hit him so bluntly he almost fell. He loved the two small people whose hair he has brushed in the morning when they went to school, more than he would ever have thought. Once when there were pictures he had helped his daughter put her hair into two pigtails, one on each side, and when the pictures came from school they stuck out in odd directions though his daughter seemed happy in the picture, pleased with the braids her dad had put there.

But now the witch was no longer a villain, possibly. People were beginning to say her life was denied, she was cheated and he feared some would see him as bad. He had heard there were those in cities who were saying such things. Would they say he had bullied and mistreated his wife, abused or neglected his children? Yes, he thought they might say, they all ran away, they had to.

After his first wife died from a sickness that in a hailstorm struck late one hot day suddenly there was only him and his two frightened children. No mother, no wife. He too was lonely, longed for a woman, wished for someone. Stella Bjarnasson had lost her husband when a tractor overturned and crushed him, half a day dying, twisted till sundown like a snake you'd stepped on, and it was too late. They say he fell asleep working all night to get the crop in. It seemed the right thing to do, the only thing, for there were no others, though Stella had spoken sharply to his wife one time. You ought to mind those brats, she'd said, when Hansel and Gretel at a picnic had asked their mother for a drink of cold water, bothering grown-ups with their snivelling.

Two years after he and Stella were married she ran off with the industrial-tool saleswoman from Frankfurt and came back seven weeks later more unhappy than ever and blaming her husband. It's your fault you stupid asshole, you're pushy and demanding. At first she had been gentle with the kids but now she turned bitterly against them and the father's eyes would change until you would almost believe he could see through tables and doors.

He had read that when the witch would talk her voice would be the sound of paper, slowly ripping, and you would have to lean in to hear. Or sandpaper rubbing —*shh sshh sh shh. Boyss* and *girlss* she would say. Linguists would say she didn't use her vocal cords and so she was voiceless. Her whispery voice makes her intimate, a raspberry voice with men. She insinuates herself into your ear. *Yess* she says *yess*, she whistles and fusses, her voice close and intimate.

The witch also talks through her nose. Hansel and Gretel think she has a cold. The father thinks he is in trouble.

THE FOREST

a lyric moon
clear as acrylic

the stepmother moves like wasps wraps the children in
wire ties up the tongues she warps and ensnares them
they can hardly walk barely talk their father does not
know what they say they are mute fall down without
reason the father tries to warn them warm them with
his voice she is taking away the words taking them
under her spell *children children speak to me* the father
is nearly worn out fears she will draw them in they will
stumble back into infancy into the forests dead to the
father and he pleads for them *come back come back to the
house* where their stories are stacked like blankets they
can wrap around themselves but now they drag animal
shouts through their throats under the big O that rolls
overhead in circles and circe howls

> Asks of frogs in spandex swimsuits
> they snap at their waists
> proud of their warts and waterlines.
> **Dunno, dunno.**

Nope, no kids round these parts mister. Yustabe but no
kids no more. Nope.

The children are cold and wet, yet they know they should drop words behind. They remember and pretend they are stones so the father can find them. Rocks smooth as butter at his feet. The father is constant. Day after day he searches for some thread he could pull them out on. He fears his children stranded on the wire fence, blue bodies strangled. He knows owls have blown pebbles into the night. He rounds them up, for they have left them in his keeping. If they come back the house will surround them with small yelps and bips they have dripped into the stones. He puts them to his ear, in his mouth, slippery as if they were in a stream they sing clear as orioles. When they speak the words will become dry and warm.

He searches where blackness stacks & bickers. And then he hears them. *vater vater* they will try to say *papa papa.* They will sound like bottles wind rubs. Their lips make sounds from bottoms of wells *vati vati, we are here over here father,* and when he gets close they will speak as if a wind were gathering before a blizzard. It tangles newspapers and leaves and voices he can barely stand barely get his footing *here here* they keen and the father slogs through the drifts he feels cold hears muffled shouts there is a strong wind from the west a strange song in the house tumbles from as if hogs are being butchered the witch's eyes poked out by night or cold he cannot tell but there is no lustre and puts his hands over his ears cold from the doors and windows the children call again and again *here here* he spins into the wet snow *Hansel Gretel i am here* he calls and calls stars waver over the darkness their faces blur & wind blows a thinness until snow fills the bowl his heart has become.

he hollows out a space in his heart for the words his children carry in their pockets to warm all the stories they ever heard or told

THE WAIT

Hungry, they are hungry. Their stomachs cramp.
"I'm cold, Hansel."
"Me too, Gretel."
"I'm cold. When will Daddy get here?"
The cold crimps them like apple pie, and they lean into one another.

They shiver, birds shaking, find a few berries at the edge of the path. They are withered and covered with dust, the ones they eat, and it is worse, the pain in their stomachs.

Morning. Two baby robins under the sprinkler, the shock when the water hits. They run under, stand under, the sprinkler, strewn leaves that feel like leather. That or brittle when they are dry, crumble more easily than cornflakes. The robins sip water where it forms in drops on the grass, rummage for bugs that must be gone.

It is October 1, 1989. It is dry, the fall has been dry. You have seen it, every one of you has seen it, you know they search for time, the last robins, hope they will find enough of it, under the sprinkler you coax summer through. Time to dissolve the brindles on their breasts and propel them down the sky.

You know they won't make it, most of them. They wake in glue, wade through glue. Already there has been sleet and hunger, you have seen it and you are concerned, and you watch the sky for signs. The lawns are full of baby robins and the cold collapses on them, inside yards a strong wind has blown them into. Thirst and hunger swirl in their china cup bones, slow the tick of molecules their bodies drive, motors cooling.

It is an early fall, dry. It is cold beyond season, and there are cracks in the ground summer falls through.

Hansel and Gretel wait for their father, shiver and pick. They list into darkness, last birds, listen for the father. "Listen, Gretel, I can hear him now." They hope he will come soon.

And then a jay. A blade of blue. Its whetstone sharpens the yard, whittles cold off. A blue ax across the grain of the wind. A blue jay opens the yard.

Is this what they have been waiting for?

Late that afternoon the first snow falls wet and frozen on the yard.

IV: Rapunzel

GARRISON MENTALITY

                    awful the way you keep me

waiting why lady chat
elaine why do you do this
you into your curds & why

i send my feathered love
the shafts of light shift & sing
they ring & splinter against
your bedroom door

against the stings & eros of cupidinous fortune
i would climb past the portcullis
its loud grating to your bastion whisper
psst what's the word
let down your hair and for
give me my trespasses

                                    across the bridge
                        dress blown against your legs
                    you brush back the hair in your eyes
                       the keys a jingle in your pocket

                    when you sing doors spring open
                                   pop like toasters

the lid lifted the id
is come upon us

                        one by one by one by one
                               you spring the tingle

                  do not stop now do not look
                                back the cup
                          full of spells spills
                            the floor rattles
                  with the fish & the frogs

                            you must not fail
                            to break the spell
                            or force the lock

Mother Gothel

I.
it is my garden he has entered
entrails stinking and trailing
men smells tangled in twine
the cattle shrink from

first the father and then
the other the young one
resplendent in stirrup and bridle
arrives on a horse from
god knows where
into light sweet as mead
every day he calls on her
a promise of briar and primrose
a swagger from somewhere

he must have preened to see himself
the stars could not be more satisfied
than is the prince with the moonlight
that in champagne drenches him
cameras shining from his neck
"tirra lirra" from his horse he sings
and the wrens listen in

he has vaulted walls squeezed
tensile as a spider's thread through windows

all year the azalea fizz in frost
I can taste him in the lettuce
his dirty hands have rummaged
the tomatoes have haemorrhaged
and the carrots torn apart
like trees at 40 below

what would you have me do
every minute i smell him
the night hoarse with talking

II.
it is the queen's desire they feel
it thickens the tongue the young
girl the queen's thoughts
click like black
birds in my herbs
among flowers and parsley and
radish she carries the sweet new milk
the brownsmooth nuts and berries

she is unknowing her hair is
long her voice pleasing
the bright rain dances in her voice
and sometimes it smells of grass
when she sings the trees kneel
the rain slips and glistens
the pails drip with chlorophyll

her throat a blind bird song
she sings like a nightingale
you with your sentiments will say
but you know nothing of her
nothing of what she feels
the sweet ache when she wakes
a meadowlark splintering the sky

III.

every day I call on her every day
I carry the ring her songs swing from
Rapunzel I call Rapunzel Rapunzel
my daughter my lovely daughter
than whom there is none
more lovely

                all day in the tower
                  my daughter and I
            her grace and daughterliness

the world below sullied with noise
the swarming and warty world of men
the green-headed mallards
squawk and tip their bums
fear the stealthy and vicious martens

there are trees and there are banks
the brush of skin on skin the coolness of rivers
trees breathe beside and onto
and there are trees that swish
past in rain and headlights
she can see in the blue mirror moving
light as my lady's silk

IV.
she is my daughter she has grown
blonde as the wheat and tall
every night I watch
the young man wedge through the wall
                sleek with insolence
he hauls it up the ladder she lets down
her guard and seeks the confidence
his smiles hoist to her
i see what every mother every night fears
the young man who visits in muscle and sinew
in haste and heist

      feel her voice rise inside
      please oh please
      she rushes and colour
      rises on her neck
      the perfume of her body

V.
what would you have me do
I say nothing when he slips in
every night I hear him
at the narrow passageway
her little gasp of joy
you have come you have come
come in please come in
the desire quickens in her
a ruby-throated humming
and the shawl falls from her shoulders

VI.
I wait   one month   count the moon
it goes out   then back   bulges
into egg a blood splot
                        and clears
the beautiful and lonely moon
the purple birds skim

something in his shoulders
her quiet smile in her greygreen
eyes I have seen
his head distended
in purple and red
thrust into the small room
for such sin a single
finger for an eye

            I do not
hesitate where i have waited i
        reach out and i
    pop his eyes
        one eye
                one nail
        one eye
                          one nail
an eye for an eye

they rupture like
grapes you step on

VII.
I hack off the braids of golden light
he has climbed to claim
snip snip with my teeth
bite off the cord & he falls
                                     // splat
                   into the yard

    when he swings out
    on his cries bounces
    down the wall into
    a world brimming with fire
    his wails slam against the room as he plummets
    she screams and screams

    he sings a different tune now
    dangles on his yowls
    he can see only darkly now

    spite you will say i say too
    bad too bad for him and his eyes

VIII.
                a splattery thing
                two sockets open
                in horror two
children moldering in her body
like compost you might say

IX.
that is fine I am in no hurry
I am an old woman it is

plain you will pay me
no attention do not worry
I shall be all right

how good it will feel
one day when it is dozing
a gob of phlegm
full of flies & worms
dozens and dozens of the filthy things

all day I feel the parsnips yowling
hear as we speak the peas in their pods
they sense what is about to happen
how good it will be

X.
        I
                shan't miss

my chance when   as if
                  by chance
  the merest   glance

(wading through
my beets and onions
I do not   watch
       my step
                and

      squirk

                            I smash it flat
                    as a collapsed intestine
                      feel it under my foot
                      explode like a snail

V: The Bear

THE GIRLS AND THE BEAR

Snow White and Rose Red lie down together and the soft moon soothes them into sleep. Sometimes the sun is warm and their skin softens, and when they are cold, tightens. Behind their eyes the colours gather and their eyes turn brighter.

A thin lemon of moon squeezes over them.

On summer days Rose Red and Snow White go into the forest, for nuts and berries. The mother stands at the door, hand over her eyes, shade from the morning, and for the worry that seems to squint from her face. We think it is worry, a mother worries about what lies in the forest and the anxious tick in her heart. She has heard of men with hard mouths, small men who lie in wait. She watches the girls in bare feet go hand in hand into the trees—sploop into the green, and it closes behind them.

The mother feels as if a door were closing in her heart every time they pass the poppies at the edge of the wheat field. They sink into the forest, and the wind slams behind them. She hears inside her the smiles of the men. Thinks how much she loves her children, loves to bring them strawberries and apples. She rubs and rubs the apples, tries to wear off the freckles, rosy as Rose Red herself, the flesh unblemished as Snow White. She would give them anything.

When they were small they would brush cinders out of the bear's fur. Whenever the mother thinks of her children, away, she feels a sudden rush of emotion. She would open the door and there it would be, a huge totter, a shadow waiting to fall back into itself, back where it came from. The bones in his back would shove him in, his heaviness, and the girls would clamber over him.

They crawled over his drowsiness, climbed upon his shagginess, their limbs loose as noodles. They liked to rub strange smells out of him that stirred something they did not know. They would put their faces into the fur and breathe deeply as if they were in hay and the smell of dried grass. Sweet tea, the mother thought. They laughed when they heard the sounds, rumbly mill starting up. They remembered the farmer's wagon over the bridge with the geese and the hens in a squabble. All winter snow scoured the forest and the winds singed the window. All winter the girls would slide down his belly where the hair thinned. They smiled at their mother when he would roll over and sigh.

Sometimes he stood up and danced, shaggy carpet. He would turn and turn light as a robin on his feet. After a while he would sag back into his sadness. Then he would fold up, crumpled rug by the fire, limp as an old newspaper when it's wet. He let out whimpery sounds, though he scarcely noticed—for the warmth of fire, for what he felt for the mother who said he must come in, for the little girls, skin smooth as milk, who touched him tenderly. They found on his ankle where the trap had cut into the bone and they circled the scars with their small hands.

The mother was pleased, opened a room in her heart where the bear could sleep by the fire, where Rose Red and Snow White could love the bear and the forest in him.

The girls waited for the time each fall when the bear would drag his pain to their door. The squirrels who had screamed from the trees now sniffed over the ground, an urgency in their legs. In the mornings the girls watched ice begin to form on the well a shining glass they saw the bear through, ice their mother sent them to, and you had to break it to get water. Those were the days bear would come in with snow on him and the cold.

It was so clean and so new when they breathed they buried their faces, the smell of snow melting. The thick black head with the sad eyes, the rank body, the coarse hair. They liked to rub and pull the floppy skin. The bear loved when they would tug his ears.

The two girls always kept a shine in the chimney like a sun, for the bear, when he would get there and sniff.

Quick, Rose Red, Snow White, the mother would say, evenings just when night was settling down in a sigh around their cottage. Their talk went slow, slightly to the side, a soughing. They felt a quiet breath, a scratch. Quick quick and *clunk* they would unbolt the door *clunkclunk* and there bowing and bowing when snow blew at his heels and the bear would flump on the floor, chuffing, and there would be the smell by the fire warming. They would hear the clicks of his nails on the floor when he snuffled and stirred in his dreams, and memories trembled through him.

They loved the bear, Snow White and Rose Red.
They never loved the little old man.

The little old man would watch when they went into the woods. He would put glass to his eyes and he would gawk through the bushes when they swam in the cold mountain lake. When Snow White touches Rose Red it's a hen's egg, he thought, under the freckles, how that feels. You run your finger in it and it is the white of egg, he thought.

He would peer through the wires on his face and he wrote down many things with a long blue pen—words and numbers they didn't understand. There were columns and letters and strange symbols and verses crossed and divided by red lines and more numbers. They felt chilled, and fearful. He would perch for hours behind his eyes when they would lie in the sun till they would darken and languor would come into their bodies like plums warm with summer. The man on the branch, unblinking, made the dry sounds of straw in his throat. Like pennies clicking.

He was The Landlord.
He had figures.
Their mother would lose the house.
They had better be careful.
Better be.
They had better pay up.

This was in the summer when the bear had been gone for so long they almost forgot him. In those days, arm in arm in the woods, apples ripening, they could feel the eyes on them, the little man with eyes that glinted when he held them up and stood stock-still, who said they were bad, they were lazy, they were wicked when they touched one another. He smelled of flies and sour milk and when he breathed a clog of moths rose like pieces of soft paper. The girls would feel a sudden shiver. They would sit up—startled. And there he was.

He watched. He had records. He kept records and he would show them. He would show Jesus. He said Jesus was watching, Jesus knew and he did not like what they were doing. He did not like them taking their clothes off and touching. Jesus knew what was in their hearts and he had a special place for girls like them where he would watch them naked forever.

He could help them if they liked.

A sickness would swoosh over them. It would crash down their throats, down and down like the girl in the rabbit hole, until they couldn't move.

And then they remembered. They knew what the bear had said, the sadness in his eyes wetter & heavier than sea sand. He said there were little men who when the ground thawed and birds started to sing at the ends of the branches would pop out of the ground like beetles and cutworms. The earth would get warm as bread dough, as fragrant, waiting, and the small men who winter had frozen hard would wriggle up in sting and venom. They would chew their way to the surface, they would break through the earth's skin and swarm. The little men were warts on the heart, wens on the earth, and they would go after money. They would never tire in want of wealth and when they got it, they would haul it back to their offshore caves, vaults so deep in the earth not even elves or tax accountants could reach them, though some said you could know where they were from the terrible stench. Seldom would anything the little men took unto themselves see light of day again. It was theirs, the man with the wire eyes said. It was private, he had earned it. Once they laid hands on it you could kiss it goodbye, the bear said.

The bear thought of saying more.

Perhaps the girls were stricken with premonition. It is hard to tell in stories like this, and I myself do not know. It would be good to say they read something in the bear's eyes, in the way his head dipped, something that would save them from the little man. I would like to say that. For in these stories animals do talk, they prophesy too. As you know, they are wise and kind, some of them. That's what the mother had told them, if you love and care for them. She had read quite a few stories and she knew this to be true, knew it in her heart.

When the bear is released from his spell and is revealed as a prince, or at least a rather good-looking man with a well-connected brother, I might release the young women into the stories you and I as children have read. I have also thought of updating the story. I could turn Snow White and Rose Red away from the prince, who as a bear had treated them tenderly, who had drawn out their love for the wild they had smelled in him. They could turn their backs on the bear with the muskiness and the sad eyes who should or should not, did or did not, help them. Some may wish it so.

I do not know what to do. Would you wish me to repudiate the bear, who loves the girls, the girls who love one another, who love the bear, who loves the mother, who loves the girls and the bear? The girls who love the mother? You who love the mother, the girls, the bear?

Do you wonder, if they could see you on the other side of the page, would they love you too?

THE BEAR AND THE FROG

bear empties
a pail full of pebbles
seeds coated with honey

        all night the albino frog
        feeds on them
        by morning has cleared the garden

    every night bear
    paddles back /splashes
    grains across the sky

        which seeing frog gorges herself
    the pills shimmer
    in her they sleep

          bear rips frog open
        hauls out mounds of pearls
        fills his mouth hungrily
            licks frog dry

they fill the pail once more
bear pours it onto the ground
inside the earth frog wakes
on the night air takes them
on her sticky tongue

frog likes   the feel of them
when they swim   inside her
likes the way   all day
they warm and   purl
until her body is   fogged with stars

even likes when at dark she breaks
open and
spills them
wet & shining
into the garden

VI: The Frog and the Princess

SHE KISSETH THE AMPHIBIAN

you wad of phlegm
cold stomach in a leper's song
when you leap the water gasps
the squalls splash and flush
you over and out
a puffed-up gumdrop
wretched lump of dough you
could use a little sun

 (& that is why i
                    can hard
    ly breathe when you press cold
         cream kisses
with that flabby puss of yours
splat a few brandy kisses

you are quite the armful
a terrible gut that drags and leaves
something to be desired oh inflated man
on the moon mons

veneris of my dreams
      your inkish scarcely
          english breath
             your heavy
         breathing i wld take you
              home   & keep   in the dark
where you would grow into a giant mushroom
knob and stem promising a better tomorrow

who cares about your watery ambitions
the distant shore what does it matter
you are an aqueous creature
all sloop and palpitation

if in my stocking i were to land & stroke you
don't move id say i got you
     covered you old rogue you rogue
       when i flip
my lighter i miss
              & want you crazy
whenever you and your kooky arms
     reach to hold somebody new

THE FATHER, AGHAST, CONTEMPLATES HER CHOICES

my god where'd she latch onto this one

makes the one who whinnied & shat
in the vestibule look good
what does she see in the greased-up rubber
he's a goddamn bag of mush

the one that swam all teeth
in his yellow claws & yellow piss
he was a sweetheart
alongside this one

all's he can do is sit there
in a plastic raincoat

so how are the folks yr tryn
make the kid feel at home
ya like school
swimming maybe

he squats & his throat goes loose
I've seen more charm in guacamole
                        & a lot more gumption

that & his tongue he's got a few
tricks with his tongue he can pick flies
out of your ear at 5 feet fleas from your head
he actually can   sshSTKK & that's it
a girl can attest to that

nonsense that's his shtick
& it makes me sick
all feet & stomach clambering over the plates
it's lurch & slurp lurch & slurp
all over my daughter's admiration & her bodice
the little prick gussied up till he's full of it
one prick & he'd explode
blown a tire on a washed-out road

my god at night you can't sleep
you can hear him coming *splitsch*
sPlatch splittSSH SpLLaTSHH
he's coming down the hall
on his way to my daughter's bed

all night long the shudders & cries
till this mournful wail breaks out
in the morning my daughter shaky with
exhaustion
trails from her shoulder a smell
of coal oil & carbon monoxide
& this green-eyed puffed-up pimple
squishing behind and popping
his tongue in & out in & out
like a hopped-up yo-yo

THE FATHER CONFERS WITH THE QUEEN

well whaddaya think
mmnm

whadya think
about what dear
the shrunk-up water bottle the gruel in the wet suit

you mean the new boyfriend
yes

I thought him rather cute actually, the way he's squeezed himself into that shiny emerald lederhosen. I am rather taken with him. I think gumdrop. He is a melted gumdrop, the way he sticks to things. He does have a sticktoitness, you have to admit. That is something in his favour, is it not? He is rather sweet.

Gumdrop, gumdrop, my god woman it's a burp trapped in gumbo, a fart in gumboots. He's a bloated turd. You want that for Chrissie, your little girl stuck with a clot of phlegm the rest of her life, that's it, that's what you want? For chrissake Amanda. You can't trust the little sack of shit. Bloody hell, he'll eat the Royal Kitchen into poverty.

Oh surely you exaggerate, my dear. He does have a fine leg, don't you think? And voice. Something could be done with that voice. A future in music perhaps, there's something in that, surely. You are the king, could you not arrange a little part? You can hear for yourself the boy is pure vowel, Richard. Many's the time you said so yourself.

Him? Call that a vowel? Bowel is more like it, no end to howl and belch. Hums about as well as Himmler. Look Lenore, he's a run-away gland, that's all. You don't have to clean up but the servants are bitching and we're about to lose our best cook. Listen to reason, woman. One minute he's a face bulging with goggles, you think it's glamorous, he's a famous race driver. I say it's glaucoma, through & through. I pray he'll croak, the little prick—nothing but gulp & slosh. Seen more get-up-and-go in a guppy & yr talkin wedding. By the sweet balls of Beelzebub woman.

Well that simply is not true dear. He blends in so well, he would fit in so nicely. You hardly notice him on the snooker table.

Right. And he don't care a lick about cricket.

You could befriend him you know.
For Chrissie's sake.
It's been done.
Before.
It's not out of the question.

Nuts to that Madeline. It's a snap bean escaped from the patch. A blown-up leaf of spinach.

On the mantle, there. It amuses me, Richard, the way

he sleeps and pop, just like that, that long long tongue. I rather fancy him then, those moments. I'd imagine Chrissie likes it. He is rather fetching: Mickey on that mantle there, back to the wall, ready to leap. Bright shining as the sun.

the king: Pop, nothing. It's gurgle and poop, it's rheumy and stupid. It's an appetite slung around an anus, and a filthy taste for bugs.

the queen: he could be a grommet in the castle, oh Richard you silly he would never stray far. He is quite the gentleman when he sploops into the pool. Is there nothing for him at the Royal Baths?

king: Good form, my ass. Only thing he's good for, the little grunt, is toilet plunger at the officer's mess.

queen: No, I simply will not hear this. That wonderful Mr. Arnason who knows all about these things from his days at Gimli says he's quite remarkable at the pool, a fine young swimmer. A natural. And that is the end of it. I will not hear another word.

                              queen:

                    king:

                              queen:
                    queen:
                              queen:

                                        queen:
                                  king:

         queen:

                 queen : : :
                              : : :

THE FROG & THE PRINCESS

✱

frog she says *you're a frog*
& there is a resemblance (small)

she remembers the sounds he makes
when he swims the swampy darkness
drifts on blinks and burps

mating calls he says shaking
mating calls is what
they are i am a frog & you move

closer than a mud hen
        suddenly
to kiss

✱

badly muddled he looks
in the mirror in the morning
for weeks he waits for it

to take effect
mopes in his green blotches
hopes it will never lose
        its magic

❋

true frogs are streamlined with bullet bodies and pointy heads they have big eardrums bulging eyes and toes covered with skin and legs well-developed legs ladies allow will make prodigious leaps in escaping danger or jumping into places on a sticky tongue

❋

    he climbs from sleep
    rattles wind chimes & green rain
    his limbs are glowing with love
            the princess knows
    the charm will never
           wear off

❋

        he is awfully soggy
        sad & lonely as a guppy
        he yanks & yawps at flies

        what romance what chance
        this will amount to anything
        the banks of night are slippery
        with possibilities she knows

she may lose
her footing and fall in but she
stoops leans toward
the beer-bottle brown in his eyes

gives him a good one
plants one wet smacker /whack
wetter than a mackerel

✖

what will they say when
aghast she pulls back
from his long legs

throws him splat against
the wall of night

VII: Goldilocks

GOLDILOCKS

you have heard it all before there are three bowls round
as hope birds call to her goldilocks they call goldilocks
again and again goldilocks full of porridge there is a
young girl a frightened partridge always there is a young
girl a young girl goes into the woods she sees they are
wild they are wired with wolves & bears & singles bars
& short little men with long beards & czechoslovakian
accents glow weirdly even at dawn they are running over
the lawn with freon strawberries but the young girl is not
worried she eats them easy as cheese chooses the freshest
berries & slaps mosquitoes

she is blonde always she is young only this time she is not
she is older & she is married or she was or will be & she
goes into the forests where pigeons talk to her & to one
another & pigs do too & she does not fall asleep on a mat
of moss she peers over cliffs where waters swish & there
she meets

one who is blond or brunette or red & she likes strawber-
ries a strawberry blonde then or not though we cannot
tell she likes cream, new cream on her berries, and some-
times she likes to run her fingers lightly up & down up &
down her silk stockings her legs feel slippery as water as
wind at night when cool comes off in grains of sand the
tanned man turns like a vigil on the path bluer than the
shoulder of air he pushes heavily and the light slips off
him like rain he glistens & sun goes heavy

with syrup their skin feels the scratches she took from
brambles the air holds the smells from under hold her
breath thickens the pheromones the light in new lumber
becomes amber a dangle of sun on raspberries sweetsour
her tongue breaks the seeds and juices and saskatoons
gather in a honey pail

please she thinks it is bear please let it be bear her lips
feel funny

it always is this way she loses herself in the forest the
frost scratches her face & she seeks a warmth that crawls
inside & curls up for the night the small scratch that will
flower and stockings that crinkle but always it is late it
is too hot or too cold too soft or too hard in the shaggy
darkness it is too big or too small the food the chairs the
bed leave her squirming & restless the feeling floods her
there must be something tonight is she lucky tonight if
she is sleeping in a bed some place where ants float on
bear's breath a strange tongue at the small of her back she
must close her eyes feel the warm smell of light & honey
he whispers in her ear

VIII: SNOW WHITE

MIRROR

❋

when you look
to the mirror
you can see
she is back
she is crowblack
her cheeks tomato-red
her skin whiter than edelweiss
her face cool people said
as the creek from the mountains
pure as milk from the royal dairy

❋

she flees into the black
film throws her
in silver jerks beasts lurch
their purple mouths make grating sounds
they heave past in ebony whips
her lips wet and glossy

✶

always the blue mirror the Queen lives behind
knows she will leave behind
her beauty squeezed like a lemon

The mirror is an egg, gold-framed. It could be a compact
the Queen opens to catch or chalk her face. The hinges
shut with a chunk like a paper cutter.

She begins to feel she is limestone.

Mirror mirror she says who is and who is not the mirror
the minor who in all the land is? Who the most of all?
She has made a compact with someone on the other side
of silver, whose light & shadow move quick as spiders.

There, the mirror should have said.
Look into the mirror.
It is you.

        always the mirror   tells her over
          & over again the   shadows quick
            silver come &   go
               in streaks   creep up
                 the face she
                vanishes inside

The varnished borders dissolve the neck and wrist shrink away

The glass eye peers. It takes her in, takes her away from herself. It takes her face and she is frightened. Where has her face gone, where have they taken it?

✽

               my queen, a young more fair
                   shines in the heavens
              rosy-cheeked in the mountain
                    seven little men
                  jimmy round her
             they glimmer like planets
             glow with their minerals
           and the snow that drifts
          when they cry the light
               falls on their tears
           shine like fingernails
             her laughter tinkles
                perfect as stars

the Queen had hoped
when she asked for her
eyes and tongue would be
a little like coquilles st. jacques

the salt & blood
make a terrible mess
she doesn't much mind
when she gulps and swallows
gags a bit on the liver
the warm spongey lungs
the blood loose and sloppy in them

✖

and still she runs through the mirror through the wounded and groaning night into the forest under the mountain under the burnished glass she watches her face when the seven men circle like planets veins flowing with potassium and calcium wake her and cut the laces they say and they lift her like a heritage tomato out of the wake when the Queen combs oil through her hair will shine redder than an incision and the faces in her mind tighten and fall dead

✖

always the mirror tells her her beauty will collapse, it will
be a barn in a hurricane a barge run aground in an oil
spill watch out there is a younger more fair by far you are
finished as queen your days drained like the palace pond
with august turned to mud and stench you are no longer
the one there is another by far

once more the Queen paints her face past the glamour
the other takes for granted the redness in the roundness
of apple the Queen gives it is hers please yes this if for
you, take it. Unblemished as a pear the girl's face follows
her wherever she goes steadfast as the seven stubby men
who bleat in the mountains, even when she feels a chink
of pain stuck in her throat, time does not bother her. She
blooms in a glass case her faint breath fogs. What is to
become of her forever beauty and the handsome young
man who has climbed through the cold rocky passes
wind whistling, his feet and hands freezing, he has come.
He forever favours her bends to her face in the mirror
growing further & further from my face, falling into itself

✖

You expected as much. You have checked the story. You have always known it would turn out like this.

You feel a surge of pleasure.

You would give an arm and a leg to see her. You cheer, thrilled, when she steps out of the cream-white limousine, off the cover of a glossy magazine, Ms. Chatelaine herself, into the aether of your breath. The crowds lean in, cameras whirl. You sigh and reach. She is so blonde the drops of blood burn your eyes. A king's daughter, always, and impossibly admired.

She is most beautiful, you say, always most cherished.

The credits roll.

✖

the stones roll in my heart
loud as bowling balls
my heavy feet dance
the red iron shoes sizzle
until I am dead dead dead

SNOW WHITE, HER COMPLEXION

                why is it
                    i must be
                untutored as snow

you would have me white with abstinence
and disappear behind my skin
the veins in my breasts blue as skim milk
the blouse a bruise on my body

                                    it is parchment you want
                                words you can write there
                                          and scrape clean
                                  scraps to be discarded

                                this is some kind
ness you show me my husband
            when you want
                a perfect complexion

   a faceless face curdled as whey
      you make up over & over
the smell of rye and absinthe on your breath

                                offer me only
                the blizzard of your inattention

winter sucks on our bones
threatens with freezer burns

it could have been sun
my love we once held here
burning our hands
buzzing in bed

SNOW WHITE, DANCING

                daddy
      unsnaps the cold
            & out hops
a sneeze from the parka

we thot was a bear & was bare
naked except for the wisp of a beard

do not be afraid the old geezer says
he too is cold
and he whisks faster than
a straw broom across
the floor the fire from
our brand new ten
nessee sipping whisky

                    why not the fox
    trot whats wrong
with the rigadoon or the beguine
the Lambeth Walk or the Pony
                        why not
everybody's asking everybody's wondering

i shiver when his whiskers in polka dream
berries cherries raisins & gold
        nuggets we call granola
his joints jingle our knuckles pop
        he sniffs & sips
the schnapps daddy gives him
           & doughnuts
& my mother's face in an ebony frame

    the little man dances
through puddles where snow melts & mud
polkas by in curls & curlicues
        in leder hosen my sister red
   rose and I smell
dog breath feel bear
   sweat we close
 our eyes you must
close your eyes
        /tight
when you read this
   try this

   on for size he is
  so light his feet
dance till our hearts hurt

he wheezes & prances the light
an inflamed pancreas
and we princesses on fire
do not be afraid do not be afraid

skin so lumpy it looks homemade
& we keep changing partners till we're in
                              his charms again

IX: Victorian Romance

PLANTING

I
(Thursday, April 29)
the garden smells of smoke and burning in ditches
the crocus faint in their sockets
the humps rise/ steadily under your sweat
           the geese string by
                      pins in their heads

II
you are dead to me
the scald in me
   scold in me too
      you cannot recall

III
i burn for this
(if i burn for this)
the garter of bones
my body a tube
on fire

IV
(Friday, April 30)
    a night of moonwobble
      & woodsmoke

you were born for burning my mother said
told of the priest brushing my eyes my heart
    its sweet ache
    a corm white & hurt in
    side my crinkle of skirts
    my gusts of blood
    littlebitch littlebitch

    it is the oil smooth from horn
    the heat on our bodies
    a blue oil shining
    our nakedness the ring
    around & around & a
    round on spools we ride
    a bone of blood

        we whirr &
        whistle the wind
        comb & wind it
        onto willow sticks
        the sweat & the itch
        of the moon

                V
                moon
                squats/
        a frog
          on my mouth

a breast secreting
                blood & milk

                        VI
                clove on my tongue & honey
            on my eyes
            i sing into
                the chill
            the frogs sing back
                        the wet air
        the thick cognac of earth

                    & then the
                sudden breeze
            chickens & dogs
                & the breathing
        hard like diph
            theria the hair in his eyes

VII

      night thumbs me open
   breaks the membrane in my throat

               a spurt of matches and
we shudder
       a blue candle
   the spooncold air

VIII

            in the morning sow
star to sperm :
      in jars i have kept

    cat on my lap & the yarn
    all winter/ rubbing
    thumb to point finger

         every may
     i hoe cold out of the ground
     small rocks in my hands

        on my haunches
        hollow the spaces
        with a spoon'

my legs shake & tingle
my hands dry with mud i find them
the rough ones & smooth ones
as if i were pinching salt & pepper
dizzy with bending
punch them into the ground

✻

peas carrots beets kohlrabi corn dill
lettuce zucchini garlic cosmos onions
strawberry raspberry pumpkin
the ground under my hand reveals
asparagus squash brussels sprouts turnip
thyme potatoes rosemary tomatoes
peppers beans cucumber radish sage

the spores & the germs
on my fingers
jewels of desire
alight in the dirt

IX

    one crow to stamp
    cold out of branches
    two robins to tramp
    the darkness it blanches

    three red birds that knead
    four shades of dark
    five black birds that bleed
    cold out of bark

    the now and the when
    in the willows that flood
    with swallow and wren
    and tauten our blood

six crows on winter tread
shred the dark and the dead

FRANKENSTEIN SEEKS DONOR

the world is charged
with the glory my friends

you do not have to know
all the details
you need only to have
a little nerve
have only to donate
the odd organ

ornate if need be
when you sign them over
or simple when you
put them in my hands

with such permissions
    I will find a way
trickier than trichinosis to your heart
    I will see
        all your fine

& private
    parts are well
        and proper
    ly looked after
    you have left
this veil & snuffed it

once I bring it together
I can make things
happen bring things to light
we could come
to a satisfactory conclusion

I must press upon you
the gravity of the situation
please realize I will attach adjectives
sparkling as mineral water

I will alter the species
the cadavers you neglect
fully have abandoned

it will all come together
one big bang of voltage

a new being and a becoming

fireflies quick as sheet lightning
purple heat   a metal sky

THE WORD YOU SAY

✹

      is underway this is just
the beginning
you are a man
of the world you keep
your word you say you would
keep mine too

                    you stand by
your word you
would not give it
up for anybody
not for all the world

✹

          tkkk tkkk ttkk
in the beginning as ever it was
               your world
    against mine

you who prayed for revelation
say i must mind my tongue

have pried open my journal
a dark lake in which you saw your name
      a broken cloud

✖

you got a big mouth you open
too wide too prone to provocation too
given to invitation and spilling
secrets you ought to
keep your feelings to yourselves
your slippery tongues
moving up and down
cheeks tongues the in and ex
halations of maybe

membranes thick with blood
with intimacy you say

✖

who's to argue
who's to say
i do not suffer

a vague but bad
case of the ague

a wicked ear
for eaves-dropping
an in-vogue ear
resistible lubricity

❋

    you're fed up
you won't put up with it

I'm in your bad books
I have to take my words back

fold them and put them
        back in their place
        set them away and
seal them with rose water
mauve linens and teaspoons and dried flowers

                    out of sight
                    out of mind
free from notice

❋

                (as you say)
we are gossip and hearsay
all we hear and say

  in the heresy of paper i look
        for something strange a
    quaint word in the ear

   i leap to the slither
of way-off words that astound
when they bounce

       off the wall and off the bones
       which i love listening

seek times that release
thoughts of some
sweet-tongued lover who has
my ear in the morning
a strong wind a shiver
and carries away in his socks
the golden powder

you being chivalrous lock me up
look it is me, bb, look me up
why don't you
where you have put me

❋

      promises promises   the primrose path
           all the way down
      the giddy infidelities the crazy rise
      on our tongues the ins & outs
      as Eve in the books we keep
      sitting up at night to love and mine

❋

we have found our sweet and sour tongues wanton
with want we are no longer lost we will not hold
them nor will we bite them nor
despite your advice will we tie them

       we know what it is

                            to have it
                        on the tip of
                        the tongue

✱

they are not civil, the tongues, they will cavil will revel in
splitting hairs in dispute unravelling clauses that up and
run off run away with us, the words, reveal themselves,
caught in our teeth our nose our mouths, shameless as
all get out we get the word out the word is out on you
mister the tattle-tale words will tell on you will spill the
beans we will shoot our mouths off bang bang yr dead
we are simply minding our Ps & Qs we will stick out
our tongues immodest and moveable they will wag take
things right out of the air make things up mark my words
talk about cheek our lips spread we strew desire by word
of mouth by slips of the tongue the ache in so many
tongues we are at it from the word go morning noon and
night time too we speak in our first tongue in mother
tongues foreign tongues forbidden tongues in other
words the babble for which we stand convicted out of our
own mouths

my word you say alarmed you say the word
is mum the point is moot we say

✲

the words we die to speak

we talk our heads off
and some times lose them
somewhere deep inside the blue castle
where you a blue-black crow
shine and glower

  coming toward
     two words to
         ward off what i might say &
        true to your word
            now and then do

✲

does the silver spoon leave a bad
taste in your mouth does it hurt
when you put words in my mouth
spooning them like pablum

does it bother you
I am wanting to speak
in a scarlet delirium

        that we have come
        down with   a fever   a sore throat

                           hoarse crows
             so to speak
        rash to speak
             in a rush
                         pleasurably
     of our own
               accord
    on our own
            say-so

✱

accordingly we are proclitic we love to find one thing leads on to another one word after the other and yet another and there can be no going back we cannot go back on our word it is rapture to play so may we commingle in shape and sound no longer married to the plain old word we love to take in those we fall upon or that fall into our laps we embrace immodest words without plan or foresight act in guess and double entendre given to riddle and equivocation where we might lie in wild expenditure with the speed of humming birds and the appetite of magpies

✖

i would give you my word
but where in the world
would you hear it
running down the dining-room wall
where is it you plan to keep it
now you have
yanked the words like confiscated teeth

there shall be no more (you say)
pleasure on my tongue
no more pressure on your patience
no more glide and tremour

you have promised you would
have a word for me
a word with me
a word for my own good
not a word of a lie

what profits it a man (i say)
though he gain the word
you cut & nail the edict
tight-lipped as Martin
Luther on the door
way to your approval

            he who has ears i say
              let him be first

                              first let him be
                               let him be first
            to listen

X: By the River Sticks

HE DIES IN THE HANDS

(in 10-part harm
ony only if lonely
if met on, o my

I
where ambrosia flowed in pizza and in barley suds
the songs he sang brought creatures in blue smoke
all beasts in halos all birds and men
women too steeped in the sacred liquid
      all stepped to his fable
          swayed when they stepped and stopped
propped their elbows on the red-topped table

                    crowded there and gazed
              his bewhiskered voice rolled and
                bulged round the bar room
              swept them away like a broom
           and they wept when they heard

II

there in conclave more than three
on a rug in raging to choose a new chief
stood critics without kerchief and with
out mirth without stop their naked
and crazed breasts in rags of fur were they
and tried afar in dark fire
to stare or steer him down
yet kept he twanging on
tee-wanging on his lips and on his hip
the strings he played his glossy hair
before those glassy one-eyed readers

III

whereat the chiefest among them began to holler
look at the pretty boy who will not have us
too good are you fancy pants the way
you burn and turn us down and into hissing
hussies into mournful harpies
herpes would be too good for you you drunken dink
ladies let's let loose & bust his fuzzied nuts

                    she said and out of the herd so shouting
                          shot a jibe from the polar regions
                          hard as ice & jagged at his singing
went it and all who heard it said
in its very sound was it feral

IV

the sex-massed missive barely brushed his white face
nicked his moustache black as a jar of greek olives
his lips untouched were they also
and so also his crowblack songs
and his glossy hair was long and vain

whereat one of their buddies chuckled & snickered
a sneer tougher than dental floss more
iron than a spider's spit piss on that she taunted
her words somersaulted as pigeons
specially bred on slumtop rooftops tumble
when homeward or downward they stutter
on crosswired nerves so spun her tirade
into the harmonics of his country charm
by which she was sorely tried she was sick
and tired and so she rejoiced when it swung
past his face and round his ears lasered with anger
at what said he to them sweeter than calypso sang

now all the women screamed and stomped death
pumped rage humped in them thick as a hippo and
twice as massive death rumbled their boots thumped
through their jeans they thumbed
(those who had them on) were having him on

lyre lyre pants on fire

V

in bloodgurgles the pickled women slapped
their breasts and thighs clattered in seabird shrieks
and taunts soon shouted down
the poet's simple lays and thus picked up and hurled
huge contumelies scurrilities bitter as sauerkraut
disparagements incivilities beyond measure sharp
and hard as the sticks
young machos ram into one another's ribs
and faces when odin on his breath rimes water
and ice and their slaps in the face draw blood
their fingers and faces streaked they with
his blood and put the boots to him

VI

when his words could no longer ward them off
he found him then in the dark nor friend nor ear
before the howls of those weird fiends
they all began away to sink and slink
though his voice still jingled still
brightly whirled their blood the lovers of
golden beer and silver words (once his
pride to move) got their asses out of there
and yea their loud mouths too
fled in disarray from the dark and smoky cave
left the blue light coughing and rubbing their eyes

VII

now as when nhl goons
tired of mere sparring
swoon to spear and punch
drunk sparing no one
intent they should be ript to pieces
the bones stript clean
that's pretty much what happened

the furies deadlier than caffeine kathy
decided spurning's too good for the nincompoop
began to break up the joint and his joints too
smashed the show to smithereens

it is sparagmos time they shouted
time for irony time for satire
time forsaking the mother
time to beat him for good measure
time to beat the shit out of him
in this the winter of our discontent

more than ready were they
for a bout of disquietude & disgruntlement
for surely were they more than game

VIII

they had a knack to nick and knock
they could unlock and make him
lack his well-liked knackers
out of their knickers did they kick & snick
at his private parts jabbed his eyes
tuh rerrah boom tee yay
        yay!! !yaaayy
they shouted louder and lewder shrieked and beat
beat on their bare legs & bums hummed like dynamos
intent on bringing him in terror down by dawn
his bones lost & strewn over terra incognita

would they rip him limb
from limb tear him
to pieces from him
his guile & garments

it was a goddamn disgrace he was allowed in any place
said they & at his parts did they rip & snap
at his tenderest parts did their best
                    to put an end
nooky *no more nooky*
      no more nooky
cried they as one voice from chasms freed

IX

                yet his voice still thrilling
                    sends a chill through them
      why doncha want me way ya useta do
    my arms are still trembly and my hands will still do
yet grows their chant greater until it swells against the
      walls as when night ocean bursts upon the shoals
and so knocks over the little round tables with the red
            cloth tops blew open the doors

yet sang he on *when tears come thunderin' out*
and looked they then for nastier
weapons vaster cruelties
each yet more mastodonic & yet
more crazed in cruelties
why cancha want me the way ya said yuh done

yet sang he on
love's hurts and letdowns
when tears crash down like freezing hail
in and on and under tables
found bottles half full
of jeers they smashed
and in the pub broad-shouldered
bellowed they and ran at him rammed they him
aglow with smudged glasses and stinking cigarettes

the blades of ladies sla‖shed and sl∆ashed
ha!cked they at the ≥soft-bel♂lied ox
ripped sides open tore ·↑out horns
with hate withdrew† & threw them
selves again & again on him who knelt
as always before them had the lovelorn poet sang
(a song that never once had failed to touch)

X

before they boot-stomped his gibson
and blasted him a lethal thwack
he blest them all in the bluest air and
in one last yodel let go his severed head

and in unspeakable fury they threw all the scraps
to the crows in the frozen parking lot

XI

& to this day it is said
               his cunning tongue (wick
                  in a lamp
              wire in a bulb) goes on
               on its bier ringing
               up and down the red

XI: Once Bitten

HE IS BORN

poked my head
through a sky lined
with silk opened
with the small
sound of ripping a
hole a parasol
breaks round the
sun a halo the
blood falls out my
head an elevator
snaps up side down
in its timbers all
night a bird in wet
shudderings

OBSTETRICS

                              have you yourself not
                                    been a wrestler
                                 thrown in grappling
            hooks dear reader
launched into placental darkness
estuaries which envelope your dreams
obituaries in which you wrote

me off snapped the darkness from my body
hormones streaming down the sides

the issue is plain
        to see here in the gasp
                eh pen in
        sula to grasp
        thick green surges

        at least one of us
on the other end of sun
        a pulley we ride up & down
                        you would sacrifice
to a new asphyxiation

            am a red
        scream in your comic
        strips when you rip me

from the seas i swim
eternities of breathing
it is no breeze
when you drag me
up on the bank
yank me open like a zipper

IN THE FLYING MACHINE

got so's I could spiral night like a barn
swallow nigh onto morning I would cork
        screw high
                on the air
                        with such E's
      up & up & up & then

    down,
drawn into a black
            bottle & gulp
  till I think I will drown

        god I was beautiful
                      am\
loop after loop after loop

          beautiful O's &
              A's (ahhhs)
this is awe
      some &
loose E's
      (Lucy's in the sky you know)

HE CONSIDERS ASTROPHYSICS

      once we get this
cooled down there would
have to be a hole much smaller
than a coral reef much darker than
           the corral at which i rose
      at which in jeans and stetson you appeared
          your mouth an open surprise

a pigeon staring into the sunrise
your readiness to wade in
if there were a place to go

once you watered the newly weeded
the messy & toad-infested garden
    that is my heart

IT'S OUR SLINKY WAY OF WALKING

                if the truth were known
                      i have grown
                attached to my shadow

why not i am attracted to it
i love to to-&-fro
who wouldn't it so
late so lovely at night
the air elastic

                        the plastic parts warp & howl
                              the streets clip by
                                  in rolls of film
                        groan when they turn silver
                        you & a million pictures
                          addicted to the sighs

you run along the lines
your finger your whole body
Dracula Dracula you say
make words from your lips
you move with my words you say

            you say what i say
            is what i say you say

    till everything is
    rubbery from talk

                the words blip night after night
                from me to you to me to you
                            smooth as lava

                  inside the creases
              we make in night we tuck
                ourselves in & hold
        close to our mouths
                    wear the caresses
        tight to our hearts

THEY GO BOATING

        this is not a frog
        it is fog, your throat
        murky with perfume

    your neck makes nautical sounds
    a dinging & a knocking
    i swim toward off course
    of course they are wet & muffled
        most of the time
    & i have forgotten them, nearly

        you must have
        liked the whiteness
        my arms when they move
        above the water like this
            fast moons
                the clouds,   hurrying by

it has to be this way i'm afraid
this is London it is 1897
there is a dirty mist it is night
you drift in & out you

        have no choice
    no two ways about it you think
    tropical fish in a pea-green sea
    this is what you have
    been looking for you have
    found in the books you take to bed
    you are a tugboat wallowing
    in a foul & stinky Thames

                            don't tell me
                everything you think i think
                you think everything i think

i read the knock of oars
the rocking where you shift & peer

watch you necrophiliac in desire
float up & down the water

LISTEN

                    this night-on-the-town light
                       -on-the-gown business
                          it's not the torn tongue
                          nor is it the ferocious
                              calls you make

                          it is cells you hear
                    spreading under the scarf
             the wild expenditure to death
                            it is the scars
         they deposit in purple & scarlet

                    this is not what you fear
                    not this cutthroat business
                      what you dread most
                      though do not admit

                  the moist lips and teeth
                    the glisten in saliva

                  what it would be so
               hidden to be then bidden
to dentals labials glides
to solicit fricatives and nasals
                    all the spit & sniff you dread
      once bitten by poetry
        your whole neck

aching with effort

        you want to say some thing
        your throat is shouting but
            you do not know
        what to do
              there is no
        one to listen no
one to care

SOMETHING IN MY EYES

    it is nothing
           my husband imagines
        meteors falling
           hail fire rattles
to its final conflagration
in the grate

        nor is it emanations he fears
        that warp the purple wind
        and sorrow on the horizon for years
        nor planets groaning when they pass
        the sky a gigantic engine
        gasps and plummets

        my husband knows the deepest achings
        do not reach us do not
        hold us by the shoulder
        do not push anyone toward him

he does not realize the man wants something
when he knocks at the wooden doors
a perfect gentleman by the french windows
our paintings studded with crags and waterfalls

it is nouns you have fastened
dear husband with interdiction make me tired
the suspicions you suspend like talismans round my neck

it is bearing the rosemary charms you have asked me
to dangle
the perfume my breasts release

    it is a strange noise i can hear
    a wet tongue licking

    why do i feel anointed
        my sleeves scraping my collar
bone a silver necklace
        a bloodstone cold as catechism
pale as chastity itself

Mina Harker

many dogs barking
their voices so tumultuous
the earth has grown husky
with the noise of locusts and then
                silence

so total the world must have fallen
off a ledge and ended

i am red rust about to blow
off the seven corners of the earth
something about to happen

so quiet i can
hear the moon

throw shadows against the glass
the pane so shrill it surely must break
the shadows sliding down
a wet slash across the lawn
the mushrooms mass very
slowly toward me
so thick and moist i can taste

at last sleep and dream
my husband and i and i am
waiting for my husband
or he is waiting
for me, waving, and I cannot
,move my feet my hands smell

like salamanders the small
lamps dim the fog pours
wet as a frog's belly

we can hear the flies coughing
can taste the shadows at 8:30
smell the air turning to salt

THEY FIND THEIR TONGUES

it is the soft parts the throat finds
new shapes in these moments
clumsy and slow and after
eons: light , more fluent

stick their tongues out
learn to spell
death to clicks & buzzes
the parabolas of frogs
parable of crickets

in the shaft flesh bulges and folds
blood starts up   floods the air

                I
   stop &
I listen, drink down the warm words
                 , their milky effluence
till I am stupefied with message

the flight of words
every month you hatch
swish and say wishes wishes
all this to your head

when your chest winnows
air past your ear
at the fluttery gills I put my ear
my lips to your lips
inside the slippery air

the muscles under
which you breathe
the cartilage opens
the lips press together

no matter what they say you say we are
        involved in one another
   what you say to me beyond
the small canal it traces back takes past
                the tall black reeds
the windy ridge your collar bone makes

OLD TIMES' SAKE

                        you will go out in a big way
                 red flowers splattered onto the wall
                           i would stake my life on it

                          you will be gum on a high
                    school gym & you don't know
                                  how to dance

          you know better you know
            how they come & go &
              there you will be a
         mong the screws & fertilizer
              a cold-press moon
             a puddle of olive oil
             a wurlitzer whirling

Count you will say in a loud voice
Count you old rascal you
haven't changed a bit
now I get a gander
you haven't changed a bit
not in a thousand years

the two of them under the bulky moon
you & the Count shooting the shit
talking big about the good times